BRITISH RAILWAY DIESEL MEMORIES

No. 49: 'D' FOR DIESELS

D Dunn

Copyright Book Law Publications 2012
ISBN 978-1-907094-84-2

INTRODUCTION

With and without hindsight it is easy to criticise the seemingly haphazard, wasteful and all embracing decisions made by British Railways during the 1950s quest to modernise the motive power on Britain's main line railways. The number of tenders put out to all and sundry to supply the various types of diesel locomotives was somewhat naive and revealed an impatience bordering on madness. In the circumstances prevailing at the time it was inevitable that certain types would fail, and it was a minor miracle that some types managed to succeed at all! With experience of diesel motive power confined to less than a couple of hundred different shunting locomotives, along with a pair of main line locomotives, it was inevitable that BR would make mistakes. Post-war Britain was just emerging from the austerity and budget restraints brought on following the biggest conflict in history and it was something of a credit that a plan was drawn up to modernise British Railways just ten years after the cessation of hostilities. From a negative point of view the so-called Pilot Scheme locomotives and their immediate successors were a huge drain on the already tight budget handled by BR; that many of the classes failed miserably to come up to expectation made it doubly difficult. From a more positive aspect, what the country got was an interesting, eclectic, and varied collection of locomotive classes which was thrust upon them during a very short time period. Mixed in with massive closures, cut-backs, industrial strife and social change, the railways of Britain had never been more interesting, and for us enthusiasts, it had probably never been more exciting! This album presents some of those Pilot Scheme locomotives in various guises. Most of the illustrations are of the locomotives themselves either on shed, works, or stationary somewhere on the system. Some train workings are shown but these have been kept to a minimum to maximise detail.

The section covering accidents, and the aftermath of such, focuses on incidents which co-incidentally mostly occurred on the former North Eastern Region. However, the inclusion of the illustrations is no reflection on a high 'accident rate' encountered on that Region; it is, purely co-incidental as recorded by one photographer.

We should like to thank the following gentlemen for reading through the manuscript and passing on appropriate comments and suggestion: Gavin Bairstow, Brian Hanson, Ian Trivett.

Cover picture: **Sulzers D5002 and D5000 stable with a lone Metro-Vic – D5706 – at Derby.** *Unknown photographer.*

Title page picture:
(previous page) Cricklewood West motive power depot; as seen during a 'shed bash' on 23rd September 1962, with a handful of the BRC&W Type 2 fleet stabled outside the old roundhouse. Heading the bunch, D5386 was barely four months old whilst coupled behind is six-week old D5397. A 14A shed plate is being worn by D5386 but it also unofficially sports some topical graffiti in the shape of the 'Ban the Bomb' symbol of CND (Campaign for Nuclear Disarmament). It appears that all the locomotives are showing the 0Z00 headcode which, at that time was a code worn by diesel locomotives involved with driver training. Dieselisation of the Midland main line was still underway so these Type 2s would indeed be spending much of their time conducting training runs for hundreds of footplatemen whilst normal services were being carried on around them. By the time that, deliveries of the Type 2 was completed with D5415 in October 1962, some thirty-seven of the class were allocated to Cricklewood. Within a couple of years they started to migrate further up the Midland line, firstly to Leicester where they took up residence at the former steam shed, and then, by 1966, they were allocated to Toton depot under the auspices of the Nottingham Division. Eventually, from the summer of 1968 the English contingent of the class migrated north to Scotland where they joined the rest of the BRC&W Type 2s but not before one of them was written-off with accident damage in January 1966. The type became TOPS Classes 26 (with 1160 h.p. engines) and 27 (1250 h.p. engines) and worked for the rest of their days in Scotland performing various tasks from MGR to Push-Pull. *N.W.Skinner.*

Printed and bound by The Amadeus Press, Cleckheaton, West Yorkshire
First published in the United Kingdom by Book Law Publications, 382 Carlton Hill, Nottingham, NG4 1JA

On its delivery run from Vulcan Foundry, Newton-le-Willows, to Doncaster works for acceptance trials on Friday 7th August 1959, English Electric Type 4 D223 paused at Sheffield (Victoria) awaiting the signal which would take the big 2000 h.p. 1-Co-Co-1 on the last stage of its initial journey. You can smell the paint from here. The route taken by the diesel thus far had been through Earlstown onto the Liverpool-Manchester main line over Chat Moss, Salford, Manchester (Victoria), Miles Platting, Phillips Park, Ashburys, Guide Bridge, Woodhead, and Penistone. From here the route would be via Woodburn junction and then Rotherham en route to the 'Plant' works. Destined eventually for the London Midland Region, where it was allocated to Crewe North, D223 had to prove its credentials to the inspectors at Doncaster before it was released into traffic. These EE Type 4s were no strangers here in Sheffield as all of the Vulcan Foundry built locomotives came this way including the Type 3s, the 'Deltics' and those unfortunate 'Baby Deltics'. The 3,300 h.p. 'Deltics' usually came through Sheffield on a Friday afternoon when many a schoolboy would bunk off school early to catch the latest delivery. The chap in the rear cab was an English Electric engineer, one of whom accompanied every locomotive on delivery, just in case! Besides the ex Vulcan Type 4s, local enthusiasts had already got used to certain members of the initial batch of ten which had been used, from September 1958, to haul the accelerated *MASTER CUTLER* Pullman from Victoria to King's Cross via Retford and the East Coast main line rather than via the former Great Central route through Nottingham, Leicester, etc. *W.R.E. Lewis.*

The Down *ROYAL SCOT* – 1S57 – nears journey end and is seen passing Polmadie shed on 27th July 1963 with EE Type 4 D336 in charge. This locomotive is one of the split headcode variety – D325 to D344, consisting just 10% of the total – which had this distinctive front end to enable the continued fitting of the central communicating doors. All twenty of the Type 4s fitted with the split headcode were allocated to the London Midland Region, and Vulcan Foundry alone built them over a six month period from December 1960 to May 1961. Eventually the doors were welded up, or removed altogether, to prevent a draught problem which had plagued the class from the start. Curiously, at the time, none of the WCML EE Type 4s were allocated to Polmadie shed, all of the WCML pool being based in England unlike pre-diesel days when 66A had a share of the Stanier Pacifics for hauling the heavy expresses, along with Camden, Crewe and Carlisle Upperby, sheds strategically chosen and roughly equal distant along the route between Glasgow and London. Crewe became the 'home base' for the LM fleet and allocations to other depots – Camden, Edge Hill, Longsight and Upperby – were sent out as required. Essentially interim motive power for the WCML until the completion of the electrification from the North-West to London, the EE Type 4 had to show off its mixed traffic capabilities on the LMR once the electric services started but they did have a period when they remained the prime motive power north of Crewe until the introduction of the next generation of Type 4 from English Electric, the D4XXs. *C.J.B.Sanderson.*

The last batch of EE Type 4s (D345 to D399) were given centrally placed headcode boxes and Longsight based D372 shows off its front end as it waits to take over an afternoon southbound working at Carlisle Citadel station in late January 1962. Besides the latter-built members of the class, seven of the Haymarket allocated EE Type 4s from the earlier batch – D260 to D266 – which were delivered with discs only, had centrally positioned route indicators fitted retrospectively, the earliest examples being fitted in 1965 as follows: D261 March, D260 and D265 by May; all done at St Rollox works. Only weeks old, this big Type 4 has already accumulated a lot of dirt along its flanks but its front end remains virtually as new. By 10th February D372 had transferred to Camden. *A.Ives.* 5

A more respectable looking – though straight out of the box – D347 has just backed onto a southbound express at Newcastle Central in June 1961. The Neville Hill shedplate, itself nicely painted, stands out below the engine's number. The Stanier '5' was certainly a stranger in these parts. Unlike the versatility offered by the main line diesels, mixed traffic steam locomotives did not usually venture too far from home territory so No.45186 has come a long way from Saltley and onto the wrong Region too! *A.Dodgson.*

Cab side of D5385; Cricklewood depot, May 1962. Besides revealing the brush strokes of the hand painting – spraying was still relatively unused at the time, even in a major industry such as heavy engineering – the builders had also been instructed to make reservation for the fixing of shed plates, hence the pre-drilled holes and strengthening discs below the works plate. The font style of the transfer figures and letters adopted by British Railways for the diesel locomotive fleet at this time is shown nicely. *N.W.Skinner*.

A rare photograph of the first Metro-Vick Co-Bo – D5700 – partaking in a short test run over the private siding at its makers' Bowesfield works near Stockton. If this was a scene from 'Thomas the Tank' the big diesel might be shivering with fear prior to entering the real world for the first time. It might even have had some mystic foresight which warned of an uncertain future. There again, its arrogance may have been brimming over and it couldn't wait to meet its public to show off its rather unconventional, even then, design which featured two types of bogie, and a completely flat front end with wrap-around windows. But, this wasn't animation, it was the real thing and it was about to hurt! *K.H.Cockerill.*

Much has been written about the ill-fated Metropolitan-Vickers 1200 h.p. Co-Bo diesel-electric, most of it derogatory. Even when first introduced in July 1958, their radical but simple lines were given a less than complimentary criticism. Besides working, usually in pairs, some of the Manchester (Central) – London (St Pancras) express passenger services in their early days, a new and prestigious goods working – in the shape of the *CONDOR* – was also lined-up for the class of twenty locomotives even before their delivery to traffic was completed in October 1959. The London (Hendon) to Glasgow (Gushetfaulds) overnight express goods train – containers on flat wagons pre-dating the Freightliner concept – was introduced in March 1959 with a balancing service running southwards at the same time. However, so unreliable did the double-headed Co-Bos become that the meeting point of the two trains varied nightly! By January 1960 most of the class were laid-up in various states of repair and the *CONDOR* was steam hauled for a short period before pairs of BR Sulzer Type 2s took over the reigns of the express goods service which during the nine months of Metro-Vick haulage had managed to lose more custom than it attracted. A single Type 2 would have done the job initially but eventually reliability won the day and the train won back its original customers and more besides. The Co-Bos meantime were stored at a number of depots, Cricklewood, Derby and Trafford Park being amongst the different locations. All twenty were put through a reconditioning overhaul by Metro-Vic's at the former Great Central carriage works at Dukinfield (where the EM1 and EM2 electric locomotives received their electrical 'bits' during the early 50s). In December 1961 Barrow received its first Co-Bo and by the end of February 1962 the whole class was transferred there. If Barrow had ever got the feeling that BR treated the town as a backwater, they now had confirmation! For some reason, during the next four years, we heard very little of the problems which beset the class; Barrow certainly made the best of their lot and used the Co-Bos on all sorts of work in and around what is now known as Cumbria. On 15th June 1966, D5707 shows off the trademark exhaust as it leaves Carlisle's new marshalling yard with a northbound freight. The 12C (Barrow) shed code can be seen painted on the bufferbeam. *N.W.Skinner.* 9

Regular visitors to Carlisle, the Barrow based Co-Bos would tend to stable at Upperby shed whenever a short stay was required in the city. However, on 29th January 1967, when D5700 and D5705 became the subject of this photograph, the whole class, warts and all, had moved into Upperby. During October 1965 D5700 to D5703 transferred to Upperby shed and by the end of December 1966 they were all at 12B! Of course it was the start of the run down for the class and 1967 would see the first examples withdrawn. The following year the remnants were rounded up and condemned, victims of BR's 'standardisation' and of course their own unreliability. Note that D5700 does not seem to posses any windscreen wipers (cannibalised for the working examples?) whilst a large section of its roof covering is missing – it was one of the 1967 withdrawals. D5705 behind appears to be subject to having some of its innards removed too but we now know that whatever was ailing that particular locomotive was not terminal. Externally, one big change to the Co-Bos was the removal of the wrap-around front windows, found on each corner (see earlier view of D5700); these were removed at Crewe works during normal overhauls between 1962 and 1964 in favour of these more traditional and perhaps safer windows. Also, the sealing-up of the connecting gangway doors which were last used during the CONDOR period, and rarely used on the other 'Pilot Scheme' classes that were adorned with them. Only one member of the class carried blue livery – D5701 – the rest went for scrap virtually as they appeared when new less than ten years before. *A.Ives.*

D5716 at Crewe locomotive works on 1st November 1964 after the window alterations and a bodywork paint job. They looked fairly reasonable like this even the welded connecting doors are fairly inconspicuous. However, it was the insides of these rather heavy 1200 h.p. locomotives which contained the problem that was never sorted, or was it? *A.Ives.*

Optimism 1958 style! For the official opening of the new marshalling yard and motive power depot at Thornaby in June 1958, British Railways laid on a special train for officials and dignitaries to visit the site. Motive power for the train was brand new Brush Type 2 D5510, seen here leaving Thornaby station for the short journey to the yard. Typical English (or is that British) weather prevailed and even though its 'flaming June' it is distinctly dull. No matter, because the locomotive looks well turned-out, even the coaching stock is clean, and another great railway installation was about to become fully operational just thirteen years after the cessation of hostilities of the most destructive war in history. What the event did symbolise but it was not seen at the time, was the eventual run-down of British Railways goods traffic and all it entailed. Getting back to a more cheerful line of thought, why was a Brush Type 2 used for the train when it was about 200 miles out of its normal operating area? Basically, there was nothing else available. The first batch of English Electric Type 1s had all been delivered by March 1958 so were not deemed to be new enough, the much larger EE Type 4s were being delivered and either D203 or D204 would perhaps have met the challenge but they may have been considered too big, those bogies were forbidden from many yards. So, the only candidate was this Brush product which had been taken into traffic on 16th May 1958 and was still at Doncaster on acceptance – perfect. D5510 was probably the first of its class to work in the north-east, even if only for a day! *K.H.Cockerill.*

The first 'Peak' D1 SCAFFEL PIKE undergoing pampering and last minute painting at Derby Works on Sunday 19th April 1959 (when it was normal for personnel to work on Sunday mornings especially, at overtime rates mind you!). The new 2300 h.p. Type 4 was being got ready for inspection by the British Transport Commission members at St Pancras station on the following Tuesday. Note that although the locomotive is carrying its nameplates, it was not officially named until the following July at a ceremony performed at Carlisle (Citadel) station. This was the first of the BR-built Pilot Scheme Type 4s and a lot was pinned on the success of this class leader and its nine sisters. Although initially working trials on the Midland main line based at Derby, the ten 'Peaks' were allocated to the West Coast main line within months of entering traffic (most of them were first put to work on WCML expresses), spread out amongst the major depots such as Camden, Crewe, Edge Hill, Longsight and Carlisle Upperby. If anything, this two-year residence on the WCML was to evaluate not just the design but also the power equipment too in readiness for batch building further 'Peaks'. Once their work was completed on the passenger expresses from Euston, they all migrated to Toton where, for the rest of their lives, they were employed on goods trains as TOPS Class 44. *N.W.Skinner*.

Even as early as 1965 some of the smaller diesel shunters were being made redundant as their intended work was disappearing with the closure of many of the smaller yards and goods depots. In most cases the locomotives were bundled off to other locations within the region but some were sent to other regions as the authorities became desperate to find work for them. In late 1966, DM 0-6-0s D2052 and D2053 were converted into a semi-permanent twin-unit at York in order to work them on duties up to Type 1 standard, albeit without the road speeds of the latter. At Bradford Hammerton Street on 26th March 1966, three of the Hunslet-built 204 h.p. 0-6-0 diesel mechanicals D2596, D2608 and D2597 languish on a siding at the depot waiting for work – note the coupling rods were removed to aid transit when being hauled any distance. Just six years old, this trio had worked variously at Holbeck, Ardsley and had transferred to Bradford during October 1965; how long they had been laid-up here is unknown. However, all three were eventually sent to the Scottish Region, initially to Haymarket on 9th April 1967, and found some employment but, it was a losing battle. D2596 and D2597 were both withdrawn from Leith in mid-1968 whilst D2608 had an even shorter period of work and was withdrawn at Dunfermline in December 1967. The three were purchased by scrap merchant G.H.Campbell in 1969 and joined the remains of others of the class at a yard in Airdrie. *A.Ives.*

Three other members of the Hunslet 0-6-0s (they – it – became TOPS Class 05), D2617, D2593 and D2595 photographed on the same day at Hammerton Street, appear to be in employment but even though the coupling rods are still fitted, these diesels are not only on the same piece of track as the others, they are in the same boat – H.M.S. Redundant. They too would end up working in Scotland, the first two at Dunfermline and the latter at Thornton Junction, although all three transferred initially to Haymarket in April 1967. Once again the axe fell during the latter period of 1967 and early 1968 on this lot but instead of a one-way trip to Airdrie, all of them managed to find a second existence – of sorts. D2593 and D2617 were taken back to Leeds by Hunslet, apparently as a source of spares for those members of the class being purchased by both private and nationalised industries. D2593 was broken up virtually on return to Leeds in 1968 but D2617 lasted until April 1976 before what remained was cut up. One member of the class, one of the smaller wheeled versions from 1956, D2554 (formerly 11140 until renumbered in January 1959) became the only one to survive into the TOPS era and was renumbered 05001 in August 1974. The reason for its seemingly long life compared with the other sixty-odd members of the class was its earlier exile to the Isle-of-Wight where it flourished until withdrawn in 1981 only to join the Departmental fleet afterwards as their No.97803. As for the last of our subject locomotives, D2595; after a 1969 rebuild at Hunslet, it was eventually bought for preservation. Those cabs must have offered a fine view of the working environment. *A.Ives.*

Until the end of 1966 the ten members of the original batch of Hudswell-Clarke 204 h.p. 0-6-0 diesel-mechanical shunters, D2500 to D2509, had happily worked undisturbed for ten years or so from the steam shed at Birkenhead. However, during December 1966 and January 1967 all ten were transferred to either Barrow, Carnforth or Workington, their place taken by the ubiquitous Drewry 0-6-0DM. This view of D2501 inside one of the Derby roundhouses on 7th May 1961, during a visit to Derby works, illustrates what was arguably the main candidate for the 'most steam locomotive look-alike diesel locomotive contest'. A number of features stand out and it would be fascinating to know what remit the chief draughtsman was given in order to produce the drawings for this class. Was the chimney really cast in iron and was it also the sole means of exhausting the engine or was it hiding a sinister looking narrow exhaust pipe? The bunker-like protrusion on the rear wall of the cab, was it actually a fuel tank? The livery appears to be black but the shunter had only been renumbered from 11117 during an overhaul at Derby in January last so the chances are it was green. The ten HC shunters were delivered to BR between December 1955 and June 1956, in black livery and carrying the numbers 11116 to 11120 and 11144 to 11148 respectively in that order. Some four months after this picture was taken, BR took delivery of ten more HC 204 h.p. 0-6-0DM shunters and numbered them D2510 to D2519 (see opposite). The transfer to of the whole class to the fringes of Cumbria was a prelude to the real reason for getting them away from Birkenhead – withdrawal. By December 1967 all ten had been condemned and all but one had been cut up within five months of that event. Ironically, the class had been consigned for scrap whilst BR was still running hundreds of steam locomotives – the disguise had not worked. *N.W.Skinner.*

16

Although from a different aspect, the difference between the two groups of ten locomotives is easy enough to comprehend. Amazingly, only six years separated the two designs but the relationship is a bit, well Lancaster – Tornado, to use two RAF bombers as an analogy. Having said that, internally the two were very much alike and used the same engine – the popular Gardner 8L3, the prime mover inside every diesel shunter numbered from D2000 to D2618 (apologies if this sounds like an advert from the US of A). Back to the HC models, even the transmission was the same except the earlier model was three-speed type whilst and the later gearbox was four-speed. The fuel tank on this later model is now located on the running plate in front of the cab where perhaps it might have had more protection. The exhaust pipe has been hidden away behind a less obvious 'pipe' against the front bulkhead of the cab. It looks the business. This is class leader D2510 inside the diesel shed at Birkenhead on 29th September 1962. Although a comparison cannot be made in either this or the opposite illustration, the HUDSWELL plate adorning the radiator top on D2510 is a poor relation to the cast and slightly curved plate with 'bags' of character affixed the earlier ten. To the left is one of the earlier ten in the shape of D2504 which it will be noted still carries the original BR lion & wheel emblem. So, compared with the first batch of HC 0-6-0 shunters, how did the second batch fare? Exactly the same or perhaps worse, all having been withdrawn by the end of 1967. Victims, it appears, of the non-standardisation scourge sweeping through BR at the time. However, one of the second lot has managed to get through to preservation; it is such a shame that the first batch were disposed of so quickly. *N.W.Skinner.*

Yet another diesel shunter design adopted by BR was this diminutive 170 h.p. 0-4-0 diesel-hydraulic which was equipped with a six-cylinder Rolls-Royce engine and a torque converter from the same manufacturer. The short wheelbase was deemed ideal for working in dock areas and yards with restrictive layouts. And, it did everything asked of it. However, the twenty locomotives supplied by the Yorkshire Engine Co. from 1960 onwards, were slowly running out of places to work. Goods traffic was being lost to road haulage and each year railway goods installations were closing at an alarming rate. Not looking its best, D2867 was photographed outside the east end of Newton Heath depot's repair shop on 26th November 1964. The view shows off the veranda type entrance to the cab, a feature popular, indeed almost universal in North America but a unique feature on BR then and apparently it still is. D2867 was put into traffic at Bank Hall shed in November 1961, along with about a dozen of its sister engines but by November 1963 it was transferred to Newton Heath which by then had acquired six of the class re-allocated from other depots. Our subject here was transferred again in October 1964, this time to Fleetwood but as can be seen, it was still in Manchester. *C.J.B.Sanderson.*

The rapid dieselisation of the Sheffield area required a maintenance base for the growing fleet of diesels allocated to Darnall depot. Just to the north of the steam shed, next to the main line, stood a two-road shed used solely by the electric locomotives of the MSW system but only a couple of those used the shed at any one time. The solution to the diesel problem was to convert the small electric depot and erect a double-ended, three-road, shed to maintain the diesel fleet. Work started in 1957 with completion a couple of years later. Note its similarity to the diesel depots at Stratford and March, the designs on which this shed was based. On a wet Sunday 7th May 1961, we see D13 and D17, two of Neville Hill's 'Peaks' outside the west end of the glass clad building. Both locomotives had been undergoing examinations courtesy of the Darnall's superior facilities which the Leeds depot did not then enjoy. Of course, this 'small' shed could never cope with all of the Sheffield based diesel fleet and eventually a new and much larger establishment was built at the east end of Tinsley marshalling yard. On Sunday 26th April 1964 the entire fleet of main line diesels and the majority of the diesel shunters allocated to Darnall, more than 270 locomotives, transferred officially to the new Tinsley depot. In actuality the fleet had been moving to Tinsley for some days prior to the official date and many of the allocation which was out-stationed to places such as Barrow Hill, Langwith/Shirebrook and Worksop, would only visit the new facility when examinations were due anyway. Afterwards this particular depot carried on maintaining a small fleet of shunters and the local diesel multiple unit fleet until it too was closed. *N.W.Skinner.*

Although refuelling facilities had been provided from virtually the start, proper servicing and maintenance provision was lacking at many locations on BR even by 1966. This is Leicester motive power depot which had provided shelter, sustenance and care to steam locomotives since the earliest days of railways. With steam virtually banished a number of the same depots were being used to provide for the diesel fleet too. It could be argued that cash-strapped BR had spent a lot of money on the diesel fleet and not enough on its care. Admitted, showcase depots such as Toton, Finsbury Park, Canton, Laira, Tinsley and others were built during the transition period to provide a superb heavy maintenance requirement but 'local' traffic conditions still required the presence of locomotives to work the traffic generated locally. These Type 2s, there are three different types note, are stabled amongst the nearly redundant coaling and ash plants on 1st May 1966; these edifies stood for some years afterwards. By now the main line diesels allocated to the London Midland Region have been grouped into areas such as Midland Lines which roughly covered the geographical area of the main line which was once former Midland Railway territory. Likewise, Western Lines covered the West Coast Main Line area. Within those broad areas were a number of Divisions which although smaller, they did nevertheless cover a large swathe of railway. Nottingham Division for instance (which was essentially centred on Toton depot) provided locomotives to work from depots and stabling points at Westhouses, Kirkby-in-Ashfield, Coalville, Burton, Nottingham, etc. Leicester depot, this place, was in charge of the locomotives which worked the Leicester Division area but had none of the facilities on offer at Toton. The locomotives on view somewhat defy that allocation description because the Sulzer Type 2 was allocated to Midland Lines, whilst the Brush Type 2 was a visitor from Norwich! Behind D5847 is an unidentified BRC&W Type 2 which was probably one of the Leicester Division allocated examples. *A.Ives.*

Though a throwback to steam days, the roundhouse at Leicester was a modern post-war building which offered twenty-four stabling roads and a 70ft diameter turntable which could cater for any locomotive BR then possessed barring the Garratts. On that Sunday 1st May 1966, BR Sulzer Type 2 D7599 hogs the table and shows off its rather clean two-tone livery. Again, the Bo-Bo is another visitor, and was a recent (February 1966) addition to the Tinsley allocation hence the cleanliness which would soon disappear. In October the Type was transferred to Eastfield and no doubt would see some service on the west Highland, albeit at the wrong time of year. D7599 embodies the final development of the BR Sulzer Type 2; gone are the connecting gangway doors which experience made redundant. Now, three large windows gave much better forward visibility and a virtually draught free cab. The body sides are somewhat smoother compared with those on D5000 and its earlier sisters of 1958 vintage. Built at Derby, this last batch of the type had all been delivered by April 1967 – a date somewhat later than expected because the only private contractor involved in building the class, Beyer, Peacock in Manchester, had gone into voluntary liquidation and asked BR Derby to complete the batch which eventually consisted eighteen locomotives D7660-D7677. After having won that final BR order, Beyer, Peacock had built the batch numbered D7624 to D7659 between July 1965 and July 1966, the last locomotives built by the company. As for D7599, it roamed the BR network for the next twenty-one years and finally returned to Leicester but not as a visitor because it had been purchased by scrap dealer Vic Berry and was cut up in his infamous yard during 1987 at Class 25 249! *A.Ives.*

In the days when it was possible to walk along and across BR tracks (admitted with a permit, or not in many cases) without the anti common sense police (H&SE) getting into a tizzy, the Sunday visits to depots and stabling points kept thousands upon thousands of enthusiasts, young and old, occupied and happy. Such was the case at Coalville stabling point on 1st May 1966 when a group of enthusiasts inspected the place for hidden gems but found only the local Type 2s laid-up for the weekend. The old steam shed had been closed for some time and the tracks were about to be lifted, hence the requirement of positioning the diesels alongside the main line. Heading this line-up is BRC&W D5370 with D5374 alongside attached to a brake tender (you will have to take my word for it), whilst behind is Sulzer D5242 and two unidentified engines. Coalville of course was the centre of a coal-producing district and the stabling point here became popular as the years progressed; the diesels types changing as time went on. These BRC&W Bo-Bos eventually moved away for another career in Scotland. Whilst from north of the border came a host of English Electric Type 1 in exchange to booster those already allocated to this area. Type 4s came to move the merry-go-round trains which got somewhat heavier and required the services of the Type 5 Class 56 eventually. The coalfield here was finally worked-out by the 90s, the last lot of mining entailed open cast extraction to get at the remaining reserves. After that Coalville S.P. ceased to exist, as did most of the locomotives which worked here over the ensuing years. The locomotives on view today were provided by both Nottingham and Leicester divisions, a shared responsibility because of Coalville's geographical position – basically on the border between the two motive power areas. The BRC&W Bo-Bos are ex Thornaby and gravitated down to Leicester during the previous January. BR, it seems was starting to sort out its locomotive fleet although it was still early days in the great scheme and much was still to be done. A visit to Coalville on 10th July 1966 found the following present: D3769, D5273, D5371, D5373, D5374, D5376, D5379, D5390, D5393, D5394, D5404. *A.Ives.*

During the era of steam motive power, Fort William engine shed could boast an allocation consisting more than a dozen tender engines including 2-6-0, 0-6-0 and 4-6-0 types right up to the elimination of steam in this part of Scotland in 1962. By 1964, when this scene was recorded, and diesels had certainly taken over but the allocation was somewhat conservative and consisted just a couple of 350 h.p. 0-6-0 DE shunters: D4097 and D4098 – both are just about visible though somewhat shy. D4095 and D4096 had come here when new during the summer of 1961 but they both moved to Inverness to be replaced by the present residents which came second-hand from Perth and Stirling respectively. The main line diesel presence, the English Electric Type 1 and BRC&W Type 2 (complete with miniature snow ploughs), were visitors from Eastfield. Visitors is perhaps misleading in the fact that both types of Bo-Bo diesel-electrics were daily arrivals with both passenger and goods trains destined for this western outpost of the Scottish Region. The new regime enabled vast numbers of locomotives to be allocated to a main depot for examination and maintenance purposes but the same locomotives were then free to stable wherever they finished their duties. Basically switch off the engines until required again. Places such as Fort William no longer had to maintain anything other than their own small fleet of shunters and have a fuel supply to hand for the endless stream of visiting locomotives. Whilst the engine shed itself is looking virtually derelict, with the roof cladding completely stripped, a temporary covering has been fitted beneath the roof spars at this end of the shed to provide a shelter of sorts for the fitters inside looking after one of the 0-6-0 DE shunters. The turntable was still operational and was useful for the EE Type 1s on which their crews preferred to travel home cab first. *C.J.B.Sanderson.*

Another Scottish Region engine shed which played host to both steam and diesel locomotives together was Perth where, on 22nd August 1964, a pair of Inverness based Type 2s – D5327 and D5323 – stable prior to taking on a northbound working which would take them back home. Both of the Bo-Bos had been put into traffic at Haymarket in June and May 1959 respectively. D5323 moved on to Inverness in July 1960 whilst D5327 went to 60A in June 1961. Both became members of Class 26. On the left three diesel shunters of Barclay design, and headed by D2412, with D2411 and D2444 behind, represent a class of shunter which was based exclusively in Scotland for the whole of its life. Ten of the original thirty-five became Class 06 with the last few examples working until 1981. D2412 was not amongst those few and was an early casualty being condemned in June 1968 at Dundee. None of this trio had started life at Perth, D2411 and D2412 being put into traffic at Inverness in September 1958, but both transferred to Perth in October 1963. In December 1965, chasing any suitable work, the pair moved to Dundee. D2444 was one of the ten which was renumbered and became 06010 in December 1974, just six months before withdrawal. Visible over the roofs of the Type 2s is one of the troublesome North British Type 2s, Eastfield's D6123, with an equally inglorious Park Royal four-wheel railbus, SC79973, for company. *A.Ives.*

Straight out of the box, BR 350 h.p. 0-6-0 DE shunter D3614 stands at Darlington shed on Saturday 12th July 1958 after being released from works during the previous Wednesday. Having already performed the necessary 'trials' during the few days 51A had run-in the diesel, it was now ready to be hauled south to its intended depot at Retford. 36E was to be its home for the next seven years and on the closure of that shed, Lincoln would acquire its services until its withdrawal in March 1969. Like other Darlington built batches, D3612 to D3651 were all built with Blackstone engines and GEC traction gear (see also D3145 later) which became non-standard shortly after the last of the BR 0-6-0 DE shunter fleet was delivered in December 1962 when D4157 was put into traffic. Note the British Railways crest has the wrong facing lion, a gaffe which had been pointed out to BR shortly after the new crest replaced the old emblem in 1957; Darlington continued to use the 'wrong' crest until supplies had run out. *W.R.E.Lewis.*

During the spring of 1959, with the delivery of the BR 0-6-0 DE shunters in full swing to all and sundry, Longsight depot in Manchester acquired its first diesel shunter in the shape of D3765. The 'in traffic' date for this machine was 28th April 1959, a Tuesday but when it actually arrived at 9A is unknown. It was followed-up two weeks later by D3766, then D3767 and D3768 a week after that. To complete the Longsight fleet for the time being, D3769, D3770 and D3771 arrived from Derby during the two weeks ending 13th June. Edgeley shed was given D3772 in the great scheme and within a couple of weeks it was joined by D3771 from Longsight. Although allocated to 9B the Stockport pair visited Longsight for all their examinations and repairs. However, something of an enigma surrounds D3765–D3768 and their apparent 'loan' to Derby shed from 11th July to 5th September 1959! One theory is that they never got to Manchester initially and were held back at Derby for whatever reason until finally released on 5th September but this photograph is dated 28th June 1959, nearly two weeks prior to their excursion to 17A. So, the mystery deepens as to why drag four roadworthy diesel locomotives all the way back to Derby for a two-month loan, especially when the locomotive works was turning them out at the rate of two or three a week and any local requirements could have been met by that production output. Someone, somewhere, might know the answer. Irrelevant maybe but they were interesting times on BR and all-sorts of unexplained events were taking place, many still requiring explanation! Like a lot of steam motive power depots during the period in question, Longsight received its batch and basically managed to keep hold of that batch for many years. This view of D3765 shows it on the yard of the south shed at 9A where, to the right of the engine, the new electric depot was in the making. The 0-6-0 is wearing the basic green livery of the time (note that Derby painted the radiator area green whereas Darlington applied black paint) and would undergo a number of livery changes during its lifetime; next would be the acquisition of black and yellow stripes at each end, then the BR corporate blue, then renumbering into the TOPS scheme. At some point, each of the locomotives in the shunting fleet based on Longsight started to acquire unofficial names relating to their location of work - ASHBURYS, DEWSNAP, MAYFIELD, M.I.F.T. being just a few. The plates were quite presentable and although frowned upon by authority (ignored?), they were carried for a number of years prior to withdrawal. *C.Campbell.*

Edinburgh's St Margarets shed was located on either side of the main line and on the north side stood the remains of a roundhouse where many of the depot's diesel shunting locomotives could be kept out of the way from the main shed operations on the south side of the line. On 9th May 1964 one of the radiating roads of the former shed held this North British Locomotive Co. built 200 h.p. 0-4-0 diesel-hydraulic. D2705 was a derivative of the type introduced onto BR in 1953 when D2700 was put into traffic. This particular 0-4-0 was built in September 1955 with a Paxman engine and was allocated to St Margarets along with classmates D2704, D2706, and D2707. Like many of those early BR period diesel shunters, D2705 and sisters did not outlast steam and was withdrawn in August 1967. By the end of the year it was a pile of scrap in a yard in Coatbridge. *C.J.B.Sanderson.*

Another short-lived design which came from the NBL stable was this chunky 225 h.p. 0-4-0DH which employed an NBL/M.A.N. prime mover with a Voith-NBL torque converter. Seventy-three locomotives, some with detailed differences and numbered D2708 to D2780, were turned out between August 1957 and March 1961; the first dozen required renumbering from the original five figure fleet numbers, 11708 to 11719. During the thirteen months from February 1967 to February 1968 they had all been withdrawn; again, most had been reduced to scrap before steam was eliminated from BR! A mixture of unreliability, non-standardisation and loss of suitable employment had sealed their early demise. This aspect of D2753, at Haymarket on 3rd January 1966, gives us a good view of the motion and those spoked wheels which NBL refused to give up in their design, shunter or main-line. Two of the class have actually been preserved and it would be interesting to know what the spares situation is for the pair. *C.J.B.Sanderson.*

The Eastern Region too had its share of early design diesel shunters and when Barrow Hill shed at Staveley was welcomed into the ER fold, by dint of boundary changes in 1958, it was no surprise that some of the flotsam and jetsam would eventually end up gracing the precincts of the former Midland roundhouse. This view recorded on 6th April 1969 reveals four Barclay 204 h.p. 0-6-0 diesel-mechanical shunters, lined up alongside the part-rebuilt shed. Nothing much appears amiss but closer inspection will reveal missing works plates, open windows and doors, rusty wheels and track. These four, D2407, D2401, D2405 and D2409, in that order front to rear, have all been withdrawn, the nearest during the previous January whilst the other three were condemned just prior to Christmas 68'. Introduced in 1956, the class consisted ten Gardner engined machines initially numbered 11777 to 11186, they all worked at various locations in Lincolnshire - the first two did in fact start off at King's Cross but transferred to Lincoln on 15th September 1956. The four in our picture arrived at Barrow Hill in July 1965, did a bit of work locally but were gradually made redundant. *C.Campbell.*

This is the 0-4-0 version of the six-coupled locomotive featured in the previous illustration. Internally it had the same Gardner engine, the same Vulcan-Sinclair mechanical fluid coupling and the same Wiseman final drive. The one difference was the Wilson-Drewry gearbox which on the 0-6-0 was four-speed whilst the 0-4-0 was equipped with a five-speed box. From their introduction in 1958, all thirty-five of the class were sent to work in the Scottish Region from Inverness to Aberdeen, and south and westwards from Glasgow. This fine specimen, D2431 started life at Hamilton shed in February 1960 but moved to Motherwell three months later where it was photographed at an unknown date but possibly during that summer. The Scottish engines lasted a little longer in traffic compared with the 0-6-0s in England, the last example not being withdrawn until September 1981 (D2414 as 06002); D2431 was condemned at Polmadie in November 1971. *P.J.Robinson.*

By June 1964 the 'Deltic' fleet had made its mark on the ECML services. Shared between Finsbury Park, Gateshead and Haymarket, the big diesels which were once dubbed 'the most powerful single unit diesel-electrics in the world' had settled into some intensive diagrams which found them working virtually round the clock with an hour here and there for refuelling, servicing and maintenance. Their presence was such that any failures requiring engine changes were usually hauled into Doncaster shops immediately, broken unit removed, refurbished unit installed and then back into traffic - just like that, well almost. The class was certainly pampered, and rightly so because ECML had put all their eggs into just twenty-two locomotives which were powered by two of the most complex engines of their time. (above) On Sunday 14th June 1964, D9008 THE GREEN HOWARDS stables alongside the coaling stage at its home shed Gateshead taking a well-earned Sunday break amidst all the dilapidation of the steam age. Finsbury Park's D9001 ST PADDY (below) shares the same road for its mini-break. Note that BR crests adorn each cabside now that nameplates have been fitted; also note that the Gateshead machine is somewhat cleaner than the London based machine – quite a turnaround from steam days but perhaps it was just a moment in time. both *C.J.B.Sanderson.*

D5387 was reputedly the first BRC&W Type 2 to visit Scarborough, an event recorded by N.W.Skinner on Monday 18th May 1964. The Leicester based Bo-Bo had arrived at the east coast resort with a train from its home town and, during the period before its return working, it stabled alongside the straight road engine shed, in clear view of the footpath on Seamer Road. A couple of English Electric Type 4s, and a Brush Type 4, are stabled further down the engine shed yard, near to the, by now, redundant coal stage. *N.W.Skinner.*

Long before it became a fully fledged and modern, built-from-scratch diesel depot, the Glasgow shed at Eastfield had a large number of diesel locomotives allocated including nearly fifty of the English Electric Type 1s of which three are seen at the south end of the building, D8107 and D8072 are nearest, on Sunday 2nd May 1965. Whereas Polmadie had the large number of Clayton Type 1s, Eastfield kept to these reliable and very capable locomotives, the Clyde seemingly forming a barrier which kept the Clayton Bo-Bos on the south side of the city. By now steam motive power was dwindling in Scotland, the Highland lines having virtually eradicated steam workings but some of the Glasgow depots, including Eastfield, still serviced and housed many, including WD 2-8-0s, former LNER Pacifics and of course the ubiquitous Stanier Class 5s and their BR Standard cousins. It is a credit to those responsible who saw through the transition and rebuilding of Eastfield and Haymarket depots whilst both steam and diesel servicing and maintenance continued. Soon, the shed here would be demolished and a new purpose-built depot erected to maintain an exclusively all-diesel fleet. *N.W.Skinner.*

Hither Green based BRC&W Type 3 D6521 stables for the weekend at Feltham engine shed on 23rd September 1962, amidst a still active steam locomotive allocation. This is one of the ninety-eight Bo-Bo diesel electrics supplied to the Southern Region by the Birmingham Railway Carriage & Wagon Co. between January 1960 and May 1962. Though very similar in outline to the earlier BRC&W Type 2s supplied to the other regions, this model had no gangway doors for access between locomotives working in tandem. Also, the Southern preference for a two-character headcode window display is more subtle than the four-character headcode box located above the cab front of the D53XX class. Internally the two were vastly different; this Type 3 having a Sulzer 8-cylinder engines producing 1550 h.p. whereas the earlier Type 2 had a 6-cylinder Sulzer engine knocking out 1160 h.p. Later-built models of the Type 2, from D5347 onwards, had 1250 h.p. engines which were up-rated and dash B designated versions of the 6LDA28 original. Crompton Parkinson traction motors were fitted to both types, at least until GEC traction motors were fitted from D5347 on. The final twelve Type 3 of the ninety-eight strong class – D6586 to D6597 – were built with narrow bodies to work over the Hastings line where width restrictions did not allow locomotives with normal body dimensions to run. *N.W.Skinner.*

One of the dozen narrow-bodied 'Hastings gauge' Type 3s, D6595, stables at Hither Green, then its home depot, on Sunday 23rd September 1962. That couple of inches difference in body width compared with the normal 'gauged' Type 3 body is easily discernible in this view. Note the lack of overhang and return from the body sides to the main frame as illustrated by D6521. Along with its eleven different sisters, D6595 was reallocated to St Leonards depot from 22nd July 1963 to take up their work over the Hastings line but they were back at 73C by the end of 1967. Hither Green depot took on the role of maintaining the SR main line diesels from their introduction. The class became Class 33 under the TOPS coding and were the only diesels built specifically for the Region. Besides the Bo-Bos, Hither Green looked after a large number of diesel shunting locomotives of both diesel-electric and diesel mechanical types. Like Hither Green, Norwood Junction depot, also located in south London, helped maintain a similar number of diesel shunters and was essentially a pooling depot whereby shunting locomotives were supplied to various depots throughout the Region. *N.W.Skinner.*

Nearly half of the BR-built 350 h.p. 0-6-0 diesel electric shunters went into traffic before the 'D' prefix became standard for all diesel locomotive numbering. Until renumbered over a near six-year period from 1957, those particular shunters, besides their smaller cousins, wore a figure 1 at the beginning of their five figure numbers. This shunter started life at Darlington works in June 1955 as 13145 but was renumbered with a 'D' prefix some two years later whilst receiving an overhaul at Doncaster. This is the prefix as applied by that workshop in those early years of the renumbering process – a small 'D' or two-thirds normal size to be precise. With its home depot's coaling plant in the background, D3145 stands at the east end of the main shed at Thornaby on Sunday 15th March 1959 during a weekend break. Spending its whole life in the north-east, D3145 went into traffic at nearby Newport on 22nd June 1955. Seven months later it was transferred to Darlington shed from where it worked until allocated to the newly created engine shed at Thornaby on 1st June 1958. From then on it stayed at 51L until withdrawn in April 1972, not quite seventeen years old. The reason for its early demise was the non-standard Blackstone engine with which it had been built, and the equally non-standard GEC traction motors. The rest of its batch, numbered D3127 to D3151, were also early victims of withdrawal, along with another Darlington batch, D3152 to D3166, which also had Blackstone engines but BTH traction equipment. The BR standard for what became TOPS Class 08 had English Electric prime movers and electrical gear. D3145 was towed away to a scrap yard in Rotherham which was to become infamous in the annals of diesel and electric locomotives. *N.W.Skinner.*

The most successful Type 1 diesel locomotive was undoubtedly the English Electric 1000 h.p. Bo-Bo which worked over many areas of BR but started out working from BR's first purpose-built (albeit a rebuilt steam shed) diesel depot at Devons Road in east London. This is D8009 on 23rd September 1962 outside the shed building and looking fairly clean in the process. Already, this diesel was approaching its fifth birthday having been put into traffic at Devons Road on 12th October 1957 as one of twenty EE Type 1s supplied to BR under the Pilot Scheme between June 1957 and March 1958. All twenty started their careers at Devons Road and most stayed until the depot closed on 10th February 1964. There was no early demise for the EE Type 1 however. After being pitted against other early Pilot Scheme classes, including successful trials in the east and north Midlands, BR ordered further batches of these locomotives from EE to take up work in the Sheffield area. Later, after more successful trials north of the border, a large number were sent to Scotland and were allocated to the likes of Eastfield, Inverness and Kittybrewster. However, by 1962 BR had decided that the standard Type 1 was to be the Clayton 900 h.p. centre-cab Bo-Bo and the last English Electric model ordered before that announcement saw the EE Type 1 deliveries stop at D8127 in July 1962. But, the Clayton model did not live up to expectations, it was basically a disaster from the earliest days and after D8616 was delivered at the end of April 1965, BR decided to order more of the reliable EE Bo-Bo instead. From January 1966 to February 1968 a similar number to those already working on BR began delivery from the makers Vulcan Foundry plant. D8009 went on to work for BR for nearly forty-two years, a life expectancy nobody had envisaged in 1957! *N.W.Skinner.*

Another Pilot Scheme Type 1 associated with Devons Road depot was the 800 h.p. British Thomson-Houston Bo-Bo of which forty-four were built for BR between November 1957 and February 1961. The first ten, numbered D8200 to D8209 were built by Yorkshire Engine Company in the twelve months up to November 1958. All ten went new to Devons Road but by early 1960 these had dispersed to Eastern Region depots to where the other thirty-odd members of the class would end up when they were delivered from the end of 1959 onwards. That final batch was built by Clayton at Derby, an omen perhaps of what was in store for the class. On the ER they were mainly employed at Ipswich, March, Stratford and Finsbury Park although a handful had a fleeting residence at Norwich in 1959/60. Eventually all the class ended up at Stratford where withdrawals started in the late 60s. The last lot were condemned in March 1971 after a less than lacklustre career. D8208 managed a sort of grand tour during the period from December 1958 to February 1959 when it was sent to various depots to show off its attributes. En route to Scotland D8208 managed a visit to Toton for a couple of a few weeks before proceeding north of the border where Polmadie, Kittybrewster and Thornton Junction were visited in that order. Obviously nothing came of that little trip. This is D8201 at Devons Road on 2nd October 1959 basking in the afternoon sunshine of a late summer. North American influence can be seen in the design which incorporated a high short hood. *N.W.Skinner.*

Type 2 B-B D6356, on Tuesday 25th September 1962, at Swindon after delivery from North British Loco. Co. This was the penultimate member of another ill-starred class, the Western Region 1100 h.p. B-B diesel-hydraulic introduced in 1959. Fifty-eight of these locomotives were acquired by the WR, starting with D6300 in January 1959 and ending in November 1962 with D6357. In between those dates some erratic deliveries took place with 'feast and famine' taking place during the four years delivery period; in 1961 for instance, just two locomotives reached the Region from Glasgow whilst during the month of June 1962 six of them arrived at Swindon from NBL! There are some nice bits of chrome-work around those windows – very 1960s – but otherwise the whole thing looked – according to this compiler – quite wrong and ugly! To coin an old Engineering phrase "If it doesn't look right, it isn't right!" Now lets think about the real failures which dogged BR in those initial years of the diesel era – Metro-Vick's; Claytons; D6XX; D61XX; D63XX; Baby Deltics. *N.W.Skinner.*

D6111 outside the old steam shed at Eastfield on 2nd May 1965. This locally built Bo-Bo was for all intents and purposes a longer version of the Western Region B-B D63XX class but it was a diesel-electric and had different bogies, different sanding arrangements and other detail but otherwise the same builder – NBL Co. Fifty-eight had been built with the first delivery arriving on the Eastern Region in December 1958 followed by another thirty-seven over the next twelve months. The first new locomotive allocated to the Scottish Region was D6138 in February 1960, one of twenty which all ended up at Kittybrewster. The ER batch which was shared between Hornsey, Ipswich and Stratford depots, were transferred north during the period from April to September 1960. They had been preceded by D6130 which had gone on loan to Eastfield depot in November 1959, then onto Perth in the following March. D6130 never returned south and instead settled down at Eastfield for the rest of its short life. This class had been given NBL/MAN prime movers of 1000 h.p. (D6100-6137) or 1100 h.p. (the rest plus some of the earlier batch). The Western Region hydraulic versions had the same engines. Disaster had struck the class from early days, a series of fires and engine failures had laid-up many of them indefinitely. Whilst the ScR struggled to keep the rest of them going, a new engine was acquired from Paxman, the Ventura which delivered 1350 h.p. Twenty of the earlier models were rebuilt with the new, larger engine but it was a matter of 'too little, too late'. The withdrawals started in December 1967 with nearly half of the class getting the chop, the majority being the younger members which had initially been allocated to the Scottish Region. Strangely, for a class numbering only 58 locomotives, they were involved in a disproportionate number of accidents where serious damage was sustained. For the record, each of these Bo-Bos cost £75,000 and a similar sum was expended trying to keep each of them in traffic during the dozen or so years of their existence. D6111 was one of the better performing models which kept its original engine, albeit modified, throughout. *N.W.Skinner.*

Alongside the ill-starred NBL Type 2 at Eastfield shed on that Sunday in May 1965 was a gathering of the more successful BRC&W Type 2s which Scottish Region possessed. According to the photographer's notes, D5359 and D5367 are centre-stage with two more members on road No.6. All, it will be noted, were fitted with the three-piece snow plough equipment which was permanently fitted throughout the year. None of the diesels appear to have been cleaned for some time, Eastfield then lacked the drive-through washing plant which kept some of the dirt and grime subdued even if it was unkind to the paint finish. These two Bo-Bos became Class 27 under the TOPS scheme and remained loyal to Scottish rails throughout their lives. *N.W.Skinner.*

The stabling point created for the diesels at the east end of Gateshead shed is shown with a handful the big ones' basking in the spring sunshine on 12th April 1964. D350, nearest, stands alongside an unidentified sister EE Type 4 which has different lamp iron positions (see also D350 later!). Note the newly laid track and ballast which was a great improvement on what was laid previously and which was probably responsible for a couple of derailments to these long-bogied locomotives. Although Gateshead was still handling steam locomotives at this time, it was also undergoing a rebuilding which would eventually become a fully equipped diesel depot but in the meantime interim measures such as this stabling area had to suffice for much of the time. *A.Ives.*

Appearing more like a modern day scene at one of the preserved diesel gala events, this view inside Derby engine shed on 1st May 1966 shows a nicely turned out ex-works Class 24 D5067 with a begrimed late batch Class 25, along with an ex works Class 27. Derby works undertook major overhauls on most of the diesel shunting classes working on the London Midland Region whilst only the following main line locomotives attended for heavy overhauls: Cl.24, Cl.25, Cl.27, Cl.44, Cl.45, Cl.46. There might have been fewer of them, but the amount of spares required for diesel locomotive maintenance was gigantic compared to steam locomotives. *A.Ives.*

Looking rather tired after three and a half years on loan to the Southern Region followed by a further three years working in the London area of the LM Region, D5000 stands in Derby works yard on 30th May 1965 hoping to look like D5067 when it leaves the shops in a month or so. Based at Willesden at this time, this useful Bo-Bo was in need of a much needed overhaul and repaint. *A.Ives.*

Brush Type 2 D5562 rests at Barrow Hill on Sunday 1st May 1966. It would appear that the locomotive had just worked in from East Anglia after performing a duty which had been instigated by its 0-6-0 steam locomotive ancestors long before Grouping – coal haulage, or to be more precise, return empties. Since before 1900, when the Lancashire, Derbyshire & East Coast Railway allowed Great Eastern Railway 0-6-0s to work over its line from Lincoln to the Derbyshire coalfield, these trains had plied between East Anglia and north-east Derbyshire on a daily basis to collect fuel for the coal-starved region in the south-east. Over the ensuing years the route taken by the trains may have changed slightly but the destination was always the same. During the Sixties these diesels usually worked the final stage of the long haul through Retford taking the former Great Central line from Lincoln. However, all is not what it seems because D5562 was, in May 1966, allocated to Tinsley, depot which supplied the likes of Barrow Hill with main line motive power. The diesel had in fact been resident of 41A since the previous February. Therefore, the 32A shed plate must have been left in situ by mistake or by design. It was August 1967 before D5562 was transferred away from Tinsley – to Ipswich. From new, on 5th November 1959, the Type 2 was allocated to Ipswich but moved to Norwich in June 1961 where it spent four and a half years before transferring to the Sheffield district. No doubt D5562 would regularly take part in the conveyor belt workings taking coal to East Anglia be it allocated to 41A or 32A! *A.Ives.* 45

Also at Barrow Hill depot on that day in May 1966 were a brace of new EE Type 1s in the shape of D8132 and D8133. Barely a month old the pair had been sent here with others, including some new Beyer-Peacock built Sulzer Type 2s, to allow the resident Clayton Type 1 Bo-Bos to be transferred to Scotland where the bulk of that ill-fated class already worked. These EE Type 1s were not much different from their much older sisters and had just a few refinements over the earlier batch such as the headcode box at either end replacing the discs. *A.Ives.*

Not just the last diesel locomotive but also the last locomotive built at Darlington works. BR Sulzer Type 2 Bo-Bo D7597 stands on the yard on 9th August 1964, after undergoing road tests. Note the 3Z88 headcode which was a regular code for diesels undergoing road testing from Darlington. Destined for Toton depot, this locomotive entered traffic six days later and started a career which would last nearly nineteen years and would see it renumbered 25247 in the TOPS scheme. August 1964 was a bitter-sweet period for the personnel at Darlington besides turning out their last new locomotive they had started the rundown to complete closure of the locomotive works in 1966. Alongside the Type 2 is Dundee based V2 No.60844 which was ready to be hauled into the shops and given a Casual Heavy repair to sort out some derailment damage. Another Darlington product from another era, the V2 left the works eight weeks later and continued in service for another year before withdrawal. *N.W.Skinner.*

Now this was what the diesel locomotive was all about. 350 h.p. DES D3566 is stabled at Morecambe on Saturday 10th June 1967 after the driver has simply switched the engine off and gone home. The locomotive would wait patiently until the next day, or more likely until Monday morning; it didn't require any after-work servicing (except of course for the occasional laid-down examination periods); it wouldn't need any fuel for about a week either. And, it only required one man to operate it. This shunter was out-stationed from Carnforth, a new arrival there in January 1967 after transfer from Upperby. D3566 was already eight years old when this sleepy scene was recorded but its working week was far from busy, steady would be a reasonable description. Of course, these out-station duties were shared and at the completion of a certain time interval the 0-6-0DE would return to Carnforth and be relieved on the Morecambe duty by a sister engine. *A.Ives.*

One of the Percy Main based 350 h.p. 0-6-0DE shunters, D3324, receives the final touches of paint after a General overhaul at Darlington works. The date is 26th June 1965, a Saturday afternoon to be precise, when enthusiasts visited the works and the tasks of Saturday morning had been left in limbo by the BR workforce until first thing Monday. By now, Darlington was applying the correct (left-facing) BR crest and this locomotive was in the final BR style of Brunswick green with red buffer beams, black beneath the running plate, with black and yellow 'wasp' stripes painted on each end. The next colour scheme will entail BR blue, a period of BR livery which many regarded as both uninspiring and downright boring. This diesel was built at Darlington and was put into traffic at Percy Main during November 1956, as No.13324, in a smart black livery. Transferring to Heaton in December 1958, it moved on to Gateshead six months later. In March 1960 after a heavy overhaul at Darlington, it was renumbered to D3324. In June 1963 the 0-6-0DE was re-allocated back to Percy Main (this depot supplied shunting locomotives to locations as far north as the Scottish border, and many other places north of the Tyne). In February 1966 it was again transferred to Gateshead on closure of the facilities at Percy Main. The DM behind is D2205. Note the Stanier tender in the right background. This would have belonged to one of the numerous Stanier 8Fs overhauled at Darlington during the final few years of the works existence. Although long associated with the building and repair of diesel locomotives, Darlington's final locomotive repair, before total closure in 1966, was a Casual Light given, appropriately perhaps, to a steam locomotive requiring repairs from accident damage – No.70004, reputedly the only 'Brit' ever to have been dealt with at Darlington. *A.Ives.*

49

When Southampton Docks shed received its new complement of fourteen Ruston & Hornsby 275 h.p. 0-6-0 diesel-electric shunting locomotives during the second half of 1962, rail traffic within the docks was already on the decline and within two years the first and last locomotives of the batch, D2985 and D2998, were re-allocated to Eastleigh shed to work around the various shops associated with the locomotive and carriage works. During the late evening of Thursday 16th July 1964, newly transferred D2998 was photographed resting near Eastleigh station. Note that the cab windows are wide open denoting perhaps that the receding day had been a hot one. By the end of January 1966, the remaining dozen members of the class had joined the other two at Eastleigh. The decline in suitable work had started. The 'Eastleigh fourteen' became Class 07 under the TOPS scheme but four of the class were not renumbered having been withdrawn beforehand in May 1973. Our subject here was one of those allotted a number – 07014 – but being in that group of initial withdrawals it missed out. It was actually cut up here at Eastleigh by British Railways in the summer of 1976, the third of the four to succumb. The rest of the class had varying histories thereafter. Two were withdrawn in October 1976 and the rest followed in July 1977. Some went into private industry, at least one was exported and a couple were preserved. *N.W.Skinner.*

Still looking fairly pristine, despite having to share stabling room with steam locomotives, a group of the R&H diesel shunters spend the weekend inside the engine shed located in the eastern group of docks at Southampton on Saturday 20th April 1963. As can be seen, the near centre-cab design of the diesel offered a much better aspect than that afforded by their steam counterparts although longevity of employment at the docks was to remain with the steam locomotives. The USA 0-6-0T in view, No.30071, was one of a batch of fourteen purchased by the Southern Railway from the War Department immediately after WWII, and they had held onto the shunting duties at the docks since, although their numbers were in rapid decline with the arrival of the diesels. Indeed, when this scene was recorded on film, about half the USA tanks allocated to the docks had already been condemned. However, most of the others surviving then hadremained in BR service, transferred to other locations, for longer than the diesel shunters resided at 71I, Southampton Dock shed code. Note that the BR crest carried by the diesels appears to be one of the coaching stock variety – did somebody send the wrong transfers to R&H? *A.Ives.*

Considering that initially the Andrew Barclay 0-4-0DM consisted just four locomotives, it seems amazing that two of them should not only reach the age to become part of the TOPS fleet, but also that they should then continue working until 1979 and 1981. The class first appeared in January 1956 when Nos.11503 (D2953) and 11504 (D2954) were sent to Stratford, followed by No.11505 (D2955) in February and 11506 (D2956) in March. It was in fact the middle two members which became TOPS class 01 – 01001 (D2954) and 01002 (D2955). D2953 fell by the wayside in June 1966 whilst our subject here was withdrawn a month earlier. On 1st May 1966, during its final days of operation, it is seen at Doncaster shed, its last home on BR. The following year a similar Barclay 0-4-0DM which was listed in the Departmental series as No.81, became the new D2956 in the July at Doncaster but only lasted until November 1967. It was sold on to British Steel but the first D2956 went into preservation. *A.Ives.*

This is D1598, or as the headcode reads, Crewe's forty-ninth completed Brush Type 4. The date is Sunday, 14th June 1964 and the pink primed Co-Co is parked outside the Paint shop at Crewe in anticipation of an early start by the painters in applying the two-tone green livery prior to release into traffic on Tuesday 30th June. Destined initially for Cardiff Canton depot, D1598 would have some static testing to complete before road testing was commenced. If all was well, and it obviously was, the Western Region acquired another Type 4. On a good month Crewe could turn out eight of these locomotives and during the period of their building programme at that works, there could be as many as forty Brush 4s on the premises in varying stages of construction. *N.W.Skinner.*

Stabled alongside the coaling stage, EE Type 3 D6795 spent the weekend of 15th and 16th June 1963 on Blaydon shed. The Gateshead based Co-Co had only been in traffic since 8th March and in true 52A style, it was wearing a nice grubby coat of road grime. Note the big beefy 35-ton tare brake tender up front, one of a number allocated to the Gateshead diesel fleet and necessary when handling unfitted mineral and goods trains; B964103E juts into the picture on the right. The North Eastern Region was a big user of Brake Tenders and each depot had a number allocated, just like the locomotive allocation. It would be interesting to know if the brake tenders were transferred between depots too, much like the locomotive stock. For the record, Thornaby depot had the following Brake Tenders allocated at the end of 1963: B964042E, B964043E, B964045E, B964048E to B964060E, B964062E to B964066E, B964068E to B964080E, B964082E to B964085E, B964105E. It appears that the fixing bolts for a shedplate have been fitted below the number at the No.1 end of D6795, but the plate has yet to appear. This curiosity arises on many illustrations of this period featuring the EE Type 3s. *C.J.B.Sanderson.*

This is the north-east end of Newcastle Central station on Wednesday 29th March 1961 as 'Deltic' D9002, Gateshead's first, moves off from a test train which it had brought from Leeds. *I.W.Coulson.*

(above) Doncaster works, Sunday 24th May 1959. Four of the Pilot-Scheme diesel-electric classes are represented here by newly delivered locomotives awaiting acceptance runs prior to being put into traffic. As already mentioned, Doncaster was used by BR to take the bulk of the early deliveries from outside contractors for testing. In this view, from left to right, we have English Electric 'Baby Deltic' Bo-Bo D5903, bound for Hornsey; North British Type 2 Bo-Bo D6114 which went initially to Stratford; English Electric Type 4 1-Co-Co-1 D212, from the London Midland Region batch and which was eventually allocated to Willesden, and BRC&W Type 2 Bo-Bo D5326 which was headed directly to the Scottish Region, allocated to Haymarket depot. This scene at Doncaster was re-enacted virtually every day for a number of years as new locomotives arrived from their makers, undertook the necessary testing, and then left for their intended depots. Of the four designs, two became very successful and two became something of a burden on BR and which resulted in their early demise. *R.F.Payne.* Three years later, on Saturday 26th May 1962, (below) newly delivered EE Type 3 D6739 and Brush Type 2 D5842 are ready for delivery to their respective depots – Dairycoates and Darnall – after completing a week of initiation at Doncaster. *A.Ives.*

Old Oak Common Hymek Type 3 D7061 departs from Fishguard harbour with a train for London circa 1965. This is the kind of work for which the class was designed for – long distance, multi-stopping, medium weight (eight coaches) trains, with fairly easy schedules. *Unknown photographer.*

The old steam sheds offered far from ideal conditions for the somewhat intricate mechanisms of the diesel engine but many were adapted to accept the new locomotives as they were delivered. In the Scottish Region certain former Caledonian Railway engine sheds had repair shops attached – Polmadie, Grangemouth, Ferryhill, Perth (this one was of LMS design), and St Rollox to name a few – and these sanctuaries, although not perfect, became the next best thing for servicing and repairing the diesels. This is the two-road repair shop at St Rollox on 14th May 1959 with a newly delivered Type 2 D5323 tucked up inside with an resident 0-6-0DE shunter. *I.W.Coulson.*

Besides the wheel diameter of 3ft 7ins., the only similarity between the English Electric 3300 h.p. Co-Co 'Deltic' and the same maker's Bo-Bo 'Baby Deltic' was the name and configuration of the engine type. The former carried two complex, 18-cylinder models producing 1650 h.p. at 1500 r.p.m., the latter just one equally as complex, 9-cylinder prime mover producing 1100 h.p. at 1600 r.p.m. Oh yes, both engine types were also expensive to maintain. D5903 represents the 'Baby Deltics' in this nice study inside Doncaster's Crimpsall erecting shop on 9th January 1966. The engine compartment roof has been removed but otherwise the locomotive is intact. From their eventual introduction in May 1959 the engines powering these machines gave concern. The first members of the class put into traffic were D5903 and D5904 – D5900 was initially rejected some weeks beforehand on weight grounds and it was sent back to Newton-le-Willows to be 'slimmed down'. D5901 and D5902 also had to be taken to pieces by Vulcan Foundry and 'slimmed' whereas our subject here, and subsequent members of the class were dealt with during the build. The unfortunate trio eventually entered traffic in May 1959, shortly before D5905-D5909. That in itself should have been an omen of events yet to come. The steam locomotive shed at Hornsey was home for the ten strong class for the first year of operation but on 26th April 1960, they moved into the new purpose-built depot at Finsbury Park. However, modern facilities or not, the engines kept 'playing-up' with cylinder and crankcase fractures causing numerous failures on a regular basis. Eventually, in June 1963, the whole class had been temporarily withdrawn and stored unserviceable at Stratford to await a return to Vulcan Foundry for major engine modifications. Nearly two years later, with structural and livery changes having taken place whilst the engines were dealt with, the last of the class entered traffic, again! The original gangway doors had been replaced with a new front end and a centrally placed headcode box had been fitted. A two-tone green livery now graced the locomotives, as carried by their larger cousins. Even with all the expense to get them right, the class was doomed for early withdrawal by dint of their small number and definite non-standardisation. Although designated Class 23 under TOPS, they had all been withdrawn by March 1971 – four in 1968, four in 1969, and the surviving pair in 1971. They were arguably English Electric's worse design for BR. *N.W.Skinner.*

The Western Region's 'last stand' might sum up their desire to go their own way and have the motive power of their own choosing during the transition years of the BR traction modernisation scheme. That they were allowed to make their own decisions by the BRB and ultimately the BTC, seems in itself a blatant waste of public money. Since 1948 the WR had tried to 'go it alone' and even during the years when BR Standard locomotives were being built at Swindon, the Region was receiving new steam locomotives built to Swindon Great Western designs built by outside contractors! The waste and the madness went on into the diesel era when diesel-hydraulic locomotives of different types were ordered from outside contractors or built at Swindon. The final insult was perhaps the Swindon-built D95XX 650 h.p. 0-6-0DH, which was redundant as soon as the last of the fifty-six strong class had entered traffic in October 1965. Withdrawal of that class had been completed just over three years later. Admitted, only a few were cut-up at the time and most entered private industry but at what cost? Perhaps the best design which came out of the WR debacle was the 'Western' class C-C locomotives which although stylish, sleek, etc., all carried names prefixed 'Western something or other' which made a mockery of the locomotive naming tradition championed by the erstwhile GWR. This is Swindon-built and Laira based D1002 WESTERN EXPLORER outside Old Oak Common depot on Sunday 23rd September 1962, just six months after entering traffic and still appearing fairly clean. Like many of the class, D1002 had just a dozen years or so of service in front of it but during that short time the 'Westerns' built up a massive following amongst railway enthusiasts with a fan base which perhaps rivalled the mighty 'Deltics' in numbers. *N.W.Skinner.*

D1040 WESTERN QUEEN, one of the Crewe-built members of the class (how Crewe got involved is unknown to this compiler but it just shows how far the Paddington tentacles had reached out during that transitional decade) inside Old Oak on that same Sunday in September 1962, shortly after delivery. This illustration is included to show how Crewe turned-out its quota compared to the Swindon lot. Note that the front end is bereft of a yellow painted warning panel but the inset skirt containing the buffers and coupling group is picked-out in what appears to be a bufferbeam red! *N.W.Skinner.*

What a real diesel locomotive looked like! 'Deltic' D9006 at Haymarket depot on 7th June 1962 in near original, as delivered condition ex Vulcan Foundry but in fact twelve months after delivery. *C.J.B.Sanderson.*

Fancy some detail? D3733 on the coaling stage ramp at Dalry Road, Edinburgh, Monday 6th August 1962. *C.J.B.Sanderson.*

Now here is a numbering style which is out of the ordinary. Inverness based Barclay 0-4-0DM D2410 sports a sort of freelance sans serif group which is distinctive, if not distinguished. This is Eastfield shed yard on Saturday 27th July 1963 so the shunter must have been attending main works in Glasgow. *C.J.B.Sanderson.*

EE Type 4 D313 (Crewe North), piloted by Sulzer Type 2 D5127 (Inverness), passes Aviemore engine shed on 25th May 1963 with a southbound express. *C.J.B.Sanderson.*

We have two 'Westerns' included so we might as well illustrate a 'Warship' too. D858 VALOROUS, still wearing its original green livery, if a little grotty, stables on Crewe North shed on a gloomy 25th November 1964. The Laira B-B would have arrived at Crewe on a Plymouth–Manchester working via the joint line through Hereford. At Crewe, electric traction would have taken over for the last leg of the trains journey. If the engine shed appears quiet, its a Wednesday and D858 itself would not be long idling here before a return working beckoned. *C.J.B.Sanderson.*

ACCIDENTS, AND THE RESULTS!

The date is 12th December 1963, a Thursday night but at a time unknown to this compiler. The location is Falsgrave sidings, Scarborough, and the locomotive in distress is Sulzer Type 2 D5099. Now although accidents happen continually in all sorts of situations, there are some events which are not particularly 'welcomed' – the wintertime incidents, especially at night. How D5099 was derailed and how many hours passed before it was re-railed is unknown but the crew in charge of its recovery would not hang round too long before the lifting and shifting took place. The Bo-Bo was allocated to York and no doubt it would be the breakdown crane and associated equipment from its home shed which would put things right on this particular night. *N.W.Skinner.*

On Saturday 15th February 1964, Gateshead 'Peak' D170 waits in the yard at Darlington Works awaiting entry to the erecting shop. Some serious remedial work was required following a recent accident at an unknown location. *N.W.Skinner.*

On that same Saturday afternoon in February 1964, Darlington's erecting shop was silent but the labours of the previous few days were evident after a second glance at Sulzer Type 2 D5171. It will be noted that a 'new' cab side had been fitted and one which had previously belonged to sister Type 2 D5096. What incident brought the locally based Bo-Bo into Darlington Works for surgery is unknown but the joints between original and 'new' are plain to see – for now – however a bit of rubbing down, a couple of coats of paint, followed by some finishing touches and no one would ever know about D5171's split identity. This particular locomotive was put into traffic at Thornaby on 3rd February 1962 whereas York based D5096 had entered traffic at Gateshead on 9th April 1960. So, the next question is: What happened to D5096 whereby a spare cab side was available for such a contingency? *N.W.Skinner.*

A battered D352 from York depot awaits repairs at Crewe works on 16th May 1965 following a collision with a derailed freight train at Preston-le-Skerne on the East Coast main line on 7th May. The EE Type 4 had been heading the Manchester–Newcastle newspaper train when it ploughed into the wreckage of the northbound goods train shortly after the former had derailed at catch points. Ironically, the locomotive in charge of the freight was another York based EE Type 4, D350, which had tumbled down the embankment and was in a worse condition than D352. Our subject was repaired at Crewe and eventually returned to traffic at 50A before transferring to the new depot at Healey Mills near Wakefield. *N.W.Skinner.*

The other Type 4 involved in the Preston-Le-Skerne incident, D350 at Darlington Bank Top motive power depot on 29th May 1965 just six days after recovery from the bottom of the shallow embankment where it had wallowed for two weeks since the derailment and collision. As can be seen, the body is fairly battered, including the roof, although no major structural breeches appear to have occurred unlike D352's broken nose. After inspection for both ability to be hauled to Crewe, and more importantly a rough estimate of repair costs – BR would have invited outside contractors onto the Darlington shed site to cut up the big diesel in situ if repair estimates had proved prohibitive – D350 was hauled over to Crewe. After a long period in works, D350 did not become the first of the class to be condemned and withdrawn – that dubious honour went to D322 which sustained very heavy damage after colliding with a runaway soda-ash train on the West Coast main line nearly one year later on Friday 13th May 1966. Like D352, our subject also transferred to Healey Mills and afterwards served BR for a further twenty years, ending its days working from Kingmoor depot as 40150. *N.W.Skinner.*

Date and locomotive unrecorded but it is North Eastern Region, Darlington works crossing to be exact! *J.W.Armstrong.*